SPORTS JOKES

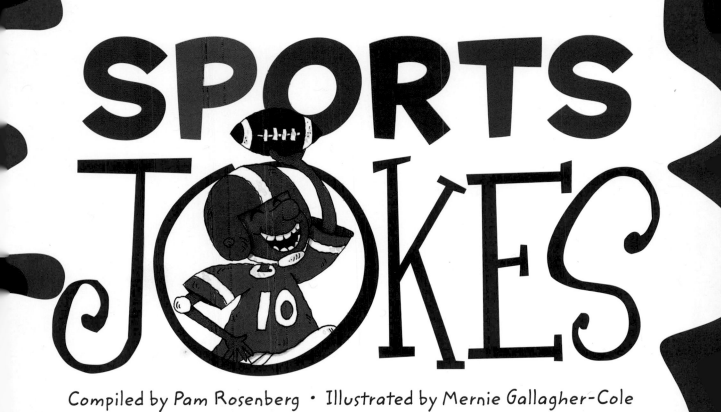

Compiled by Pam Rosenberg • Illustrated by Mernie Gallagher-Cole

Published by The Child's World®
1980 Lookout Drive
Mankato, MN 56003-1705
800-599-READ
www.childsworld.com

The Child's World®: Mary Berendes, Publishing Director
Editorial Directions, Inc.: E. Russell Primm, Editorial
Director; Lucia Raatma, Copyeditor and Proofreader;
Jennifer Zeiger and Joshua Gregory, Editorial Assistants
The Design Lab: Design and production

Library of Congress Cataloging-in-Publication Data
Sports jokes / compiled by Pam Rosenberg ;
illustrated by Mernie Gallagher-Cole.
       p. cm.
  ISBN 978-1-60253-521-3 (library bound : alk. paper)
  1. Sports—Juvenile humor. I. Rosenberg, Pam.
  II. Gallagher-Cole, Mernie. III. Title.
  PN6231.S65S67 2010
  818'.6020803579—dc22   2010002052

Printed in the United States of America
Mankato, Minnesota
December 2010
PA02082

ABOUT THE AUTHOR

Pam Rosenberg is the author of more than 50 books for children. She lives near Chicago, Illinois, with her husband and two children.

ABOUT THE ILLUSTRATOR

Mernie Gallagher-Cole lives in Pennsylvania with her husband and two children. She has illustrated many books for The Child's World®.

TABLE OF CONTENTS

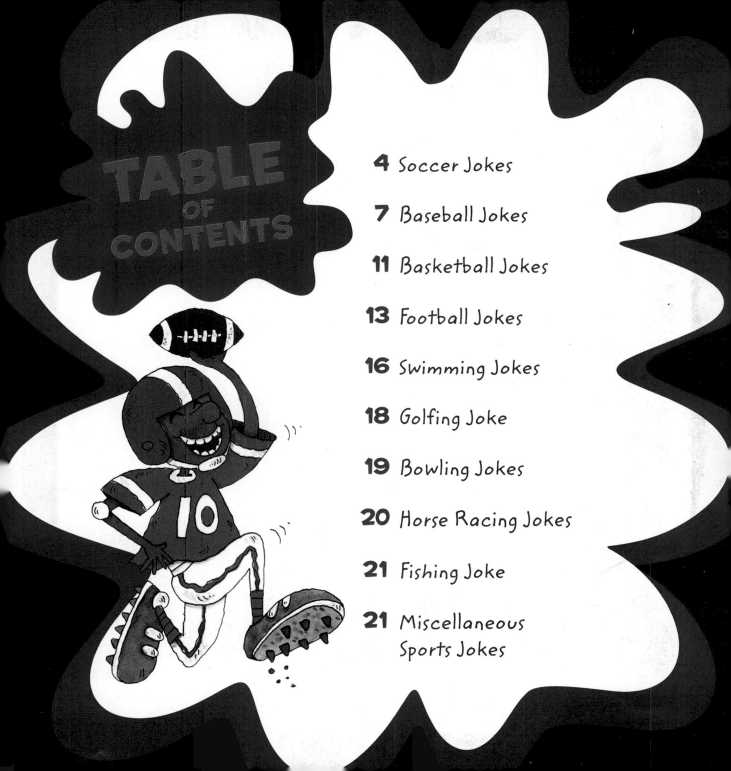

4 Soccer Jokes

7 Baseball Jokes

11 Basketball Jokes

13 Football Jokes

16 Swimming Jokes

18 Golfing Joke

19 Bowling Jokes

20 Horse Racing Jokes

21 Fishing Joke

21 Miscellaneous Sports Jokes

SOCCER JOKES

Q: Why are babies good at soccer?

A: They're always dribbling.

Q: What do a soccer player and a magician have in common?

A: They both do hat tricks.

Q: What position did the invisible man play on the soccer team?

A: No one knows.

Q: What is a ghost's favorite position in soccer?

A: Ghoul keeper.

....

Q: Why do soccer players do better in school than football players?

A: Because soccer players use their heads.

....

Q: Which goalkeeper can jump higher than a crossbar?

A: All of them—a crossbar can't jump.

....

Q: What did the right soccer shoe say to the left soccer shoe?

A: Between us, we'll have a ball!

....

Q: What has 22 legs and goes, "Crunch, crunch, crunch?"

A: A soccer team eating potato chips.

....

Q: Why wasn't Cinderella good at soccer?

A: Because she ran away from the ball.

A team of mammals was playing soccer against a team of insects. At halftime, the mammals were leading by a score of 20 to 0. When play resumed, the insects made a substitution and put a centipede in the game. The centipede scored 50 goals, and the insects won the game.

In the locker room after the game, the captain of the mammals walked over to the insect captain and said, "That centipede of yours is terrific! Why didn't you play her from the start?"

"We'd have liked to," replied the insect captain, "but it takes her 45 minutes to get her shoes on!"

....

A team of flies was playing soccer in a sugar bowl, using a lump for a ball. One of them said to the others, "We'll have to do better than this, everyone. We're playing in the cup tomorrow!"

....

Soccer players are the only people who can dribble and still look neat.

Q: What animal is best at hitting a baseball?
A: A bat!

Q: How is a baseball team similar to a pancake?
A: They both need a good batter!

....

Q: What do you get when you cross a tree with a baseball player?
A: Babe Root.

7

Q: Why does it take longer to run from second base to third base than it does to run from first to second?

A: Because you have to go through a shortstop.

....

Q: What do you get if you cross an umpire with a burglar?

A: Someone who breaks into your house and yells, "Safe!"

....

Q: Why did they stop selling soda at the doubleheader?

A: Because the home team lost the opener.

....

A rookie pitcher was having trouble at the mound, so the catcher walked up to have a talk with him. "I've figured out your problem," he told the young pitcher. "You always lose control at the same point in every game."

"When is that?" the pitcher asked.

"Right after the national anthem."

Q: Why was the baseball player invited to go on the camping trip?

A: Because the group needed somebody to pitch the tent.

....

Q: Where do baseball players go to wash their dirty socks?

A: The bleachers.

Q: How do baseball players stay cool during games?

A: The bleachers are full of fans.

MANAGER: Our new hitter makes a million dollars a year, but he always strikes out. I call him our wonder player.

FAN: Why's that?

MANAGER: Every time he plays, I wonder why we hired him.

....

DAD: My kid is going to make it to the big leagues. He already has a fantastic breaking ball. Just yesterday, with one pitch he broke a lamp, a window, a mirror, and a vase.

....

PLAYER #1: They just fired the outfielder!

PLAYER #2: Why?

PLAYER #1: He was such a nice guy he wouldn't even catch a fly!

....

REPORTER: You've really improved this season. Last year you only had 10 home runs. This season you already have 30. What's the difference between the two seasons?

PLAYER: 20.

Q: What does a basketball player do before he blows out his candles?
A: He makes a swish.

Q: Did you hear about the basketball player who's so tall that she looks like a flagpole with hair?
A: In the off season, she models for silos.

Q: What's the difference between a basketball player and a dog?
A: A dog drools, and a basketball player dribbles.

Q: What was the basketball player's favorite kind of book?

A: A collection of tall tales.

....

Q: What do you do when you see an elephant with a basketball?

A: You get out of the way fast.

....

Q: What kind of basketball nets should you use if you live in Hawaii?

A: Hula hoops.

....

DOCTOR: What would you call a patient who walks back and forth screaming at the top of his lungs one minute, then sits in a chair crying uncontrollably the next?

INTERN: A basketball coach?

Q: What position did the lawyer play on his football team?
A: Defensive end.

Q: What do you call a team of Frankenstein monsters who play football?
A: The all-scars.

Q: When birds pick football teams, why are the ducks always chosen before everyone else?
A: Because they're good at making first downs.

13

Q: Did you hear about the 7-foot-tall, 350-pound football player?

A: He's so huge the coach gave him a license plate instead of a number.

Q: What kind of bee is always dropping the football?

A: A fumble-bee.

Our linebacker is so strong that he can pitch horseshoes while they're still on the horse.

. . . .

The placekicker missed his attempt at a field goal. He was so angry that he went to kick himself and missed again.

. . . .

We have so many injuries that the team picture is an X-ray.

. . . .

The only way our team can gain yardage is to run our game films backward.

. . . .

A guy took his girlfriend to see her very first football game. After the game he asked his girlfriend how she liked it.

"It was great," she said, "but I couldn't understand why they were beating each other up for 25 cents."

"What do you mean?" the boyfriend asked.

The girlfriend replied, "All they kept screaming was 'Get the quarter back! Get the quarter back!'"

SWIMMING JOKES

Q: What race is never run?
A: A swimming race.

KNOCK, KNOCK.
Who's there?
Dewey.
Dewey who?
Dewey have to go in the water today?

Q: Where do ghosts go swimming?
A: In the Dead Sea.

Q: What do you call a swimmer at the scene of a crime?
A: An eye-wetness.

LARRY: They say that swimming is one of the best exercises for keeping your body slim and trim.
LUCY: Oh yeah? Have you ever seen a whale?

Q: Why did the swimmer keep doing the backstroke?
A: Because she just ate and didn't want to swim on a full stomach!

Q: What time is it when an elephant jumps off your diving board?
A: Time to get a new diving board.

GOLFING JOKE

A golfer was taking a very long time to hit the ball. He looked up and down, measured the distance, and checked the wind direction. It was driving his partner crazy.

Finally, the partner said, "What's taking so long? Hit the ball!"

The guy answered, "My brother is watching me from the clubhouse. I want to make this a perfect shot."

The partner replied, "There's no way you can hit him from here!"

Q: Why do great bowlers always get strikes?
A: Because they have no time to spare.

I'll never bowl with him again. After he got a strike, he spiked the ball.

....

BARRY: What's the quietest sport in the world?
LARRY: I guess I'd have to say that it's golf.
BARRY: Wrong, it's bowling.
LARRY: Bowling?
BARRY: Yep, you can always hear a pin drop at the bowling alley!

HORSE RACING JOKES

It would have been a photo finish, but by the time my horse finished, it was too dark to take a picture.

PATIENT: Doctor, I keep thinking I'm a horse. Can you help me?

DOCTOR: Well, I can cure you, but it will cost you a lot of money.

PATIENT: Money's no problem. I just won the Kentucky Derby!

Mary Jane decided to go fishing. Ignoring the "No Fishing" sign at her favorite lake, she cast her line and sat down on the dock.
After a few minutes, the game warden walked over.

"Didn't you see the 'No Fishing' sign?" he asked.

"Sure I did," said Mary Jane, "but I'm not fishing."

"Then what are you doing?" the warden asked.

Mary Jane replied, "I'm drowning worms."

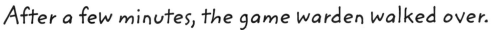

FISHING JOKE

MISCELLANEOUS SPORTS JOKES

Q: Why does someone who runs marathons make a good student?

A: Because education pays off in the long run.

Q: Why is tennis such a noisy game?

A: Because every player raises a racquet.

Q: What do you get when you cross a karate expert and a pig?

A: Pork chops.

Q: What do you call a boomerang that doesn't work?

A: A stick.

Q: Why couldn't the boxer start a fire?

A: Because he lost all his matches.

Q: Why are losing teams always so hot?

A: They have the fewest fans.

Q: What becomes more difficult to catch the faster you run?

A: Your breath.

Q: Why should you be careful about playing a game against a team of big cats?

A: They might be cheetahs.

Q: What is an insect's favorite sport?
A: Cricket!

Q: What is the hardest part about skydiving?
A: The ground.

Q: Why shouldn't you marry a tennis player?
A: Because love means nothing to them!

....

Q: How do hens encourage their favorite teams?
A: They egg them on.

....

Q: Who won the race between two balls of string?
A: They were tied.

....

Q: How does a physicist exercise?
A: By pumping ion.

....

Q: How do robins get in shape?
A: They do worm-ups.

....

Q: What's the best place to shop for a new sports shirt?
A: New Jersey.

....

Q: What is a cheerleader's favorite food?
A: Cheerios!